Contents

Rainer Behrends, Karl-Max Kober

Translated by Neil Jones

We thank Mr. George L. Baurley
for his assistance

Edition Leipzig

The Artist and his Studio

ST. MARTIN's PRESS
NEW YORK
LOC № 74-83590

It's always interesting to watch people at their jobs, and surely, nothing can be more fascinating than watching an artist at work.

What is it that captures the curiosity of the children in our first picture, watching attentively as the painter works? They have seen how the picture of the windmill comes together bit by bit on the paper. Now the artist has stopped painting for a while, to talk with the children about his work. All of us, just like these children, wish that we could understand a little of the secret behind the making of a work of art. If you have ever watched a painter you may have been surprised to see him use colours and shapes that were often quite unexpected. It is amazing to see how, under his skilful hands, something is formed that might be either an ornament in its own right, or perhaps a picture of some particular event or object, so that reality is re-created, as it were, before our very eyes. Often only the finished work shows that the artist has had a definite idea of the whole thing from the very beginning, which step by step he has brought to life on the canvas. The professions of the painter, sculptor, architect, graphic artist, craftsman or goldsmith all have one thing in common. They all work to make shapes that we can see. It may be to record important scenes or events, or just to enrich our lives with beautifully made paintings or objects. For this reason we call their art fine art. They are different from all other professions that we know of, in that they have the chance to express their pride in the jobs they do by actually showing themselves at work. So in the following pages we have an opportunity to watch them at work, over a span of thousands of years: the earliest 'self–portraits' are actually as old as that.

The Pictures

28 page 45
Gelyi M. Korshev (born 1925)
Parisian Pavement Artist, 1960—61.
Oil painting. Moscow, Tretjakov Gallery

29 page 47
Henry Moore (born 1898) at work on a
sculpture in wood, photo about 1960
from Sir Herbert Read's *Henry Moore,*
Thames and Hudson, 1965

30 page 48
Juan O'Gorman (born 1905)
Self–portrait, 1950. Oil painting

31 page 51
Bernhard Kretzschmar (born 1889)
Fire in Summer. Oil painting
In the artist's possession

32 page 52
Pablo Picasso (born 1881)
Paolo Drawing, 1923. Oil painting
In the artist's possession

Front cover:
Edouard Manet (1832—1883)
The Boat, 1874
Munich, Bayerische Staatsgemälde-
sammlungen

Back cover:
Jan Vermeer van Delft (1632—1675)
The Painter's Studio, about 1665 (detail).
Vienna, Kunsthistorisches Museum

Frontispiece:
A painter at work, talking to children (photo)

Artists' workshops in ancient times

1 Almost 3,400 years ago unknown artists decorated the walls of an Egyptian burial–chamber. Here is that part of the painting where they portrayed themselves. On the left a craftsman is busy fixing a decorated lid onto a jewel case. Next to him a man is matching up two shallow bowls. The third is painting a vase, and we can see the palette with paints to his right. The last man is putting a snake on the forehead of a sphinx; this stands for the divine Pharaoh. These artists are all slaves. Their task is to produce beautiful things to decorate the eternal home of the dead, when they are laid to rest in the grave. This tomb belonged to Nebamun and Apuki, who were overseers of the artists. According to the beliefs of Egyptians in those days, people would continue their lives after death, and actually needed to have all their possessions and riches around them. After the burial ceremony the tomb was carefully sealed, for nobody was to be allowed to set eyes on the ornaments and paintings placed in it. But the precious contents soon lured robbers there, so that only a few of these burial–chambers have remained undisturbed up to today. The stories of the discovery of such tombs by archaeologists read like exciting adventures. It was a sensation when in 1922 the English scholar Howard Carter discovered the undisturbed tomb of King Tutankhamun. The priceless treasures recovered from the tomb are now kept in the Museum at Cairo, but left Egypt for the first time in 1972, when they came to England to be exhibited at the British Museum.

The picture seems especially clear to us, because the painter has kept all the objects firmly one beside the other. None of the figures overlap. Black outlines emphasise the shape of the objects, and raise them from their surroundings. The artists of Ancient Egypt sought to record very clear images of things, so they used very direct viewpoints, looking at things sometimes from the front, sometimes side–on, or even from above. Sometimes they went so far as to combine different viewpoints within one face. They drew things in their actual shapes, and not how they may happen to appear to us at this or that instant. That is why their pictures are so clear.

2 Some 1,000 years later a Greek painter depicted his own studio. He didn't paint it on a wall, or in a picture, but on a vase. The Greeks loved beautiful jars and vases. They used them not only at table, but for keeping wine, oil and other liquids in, and just for decoration. In the picture we can see seven figures. The ones sitting down are the painters, and those standing up are goddesses. The master of the studio is given prominence by his size and his expensive–looking seat. He is holding a large two–handled drinking–cup in his left hand to paint it. His pots of colours are standing on a little table in front of him. We can see other jars waiting to be painted. Two assistants and a woman are also working in the studio, and they are all busy at their jobs. A goddess is hastening toward the master to place a hero's wreath on his brow. She is Pallas Athene, who was revered as the protector of the arts and crafts. Winged goddesses of victory are crowning the other

2

two painters. This honouring by divine figures is a nice indication of the high value placed on the arts in Ancient Greece. The Greeks also decorated their temples and houses with magnificent wall paintings. Even pictures on wooden panels are mentioned in some reports that have survived. Sadly all these works have been destroyed, so that nowadays we have only these small pictures on vases to give us an impression of how art was flourishing at this time.

How painters and sculptors lived in the Middle Ages

3 In the lower half of a wonderfully coloured stained-glass window the painter Gerlachus has left us a portrait of himself. He holds his paintbrush and paintpot in his hands, and he tells us his name in the inscription which runs round the picture like an arch: *Rex Regum Clare—Gerlacho Propiciare*, which means: 'The King of Kings may patronize Gerlachus.'

Thus he dedicates his work to God, and takes him as his protector. Since the unknown Greek artist portrayed his studio on the vase, over 1,500 years have gone by. The Greek and Roman empires have fallen long ago, and that period of history that we call the Middle Ages has begun. At this time the Christian religion dominated the lives, feelings and thoughts of men. They built thousands of churches, both great and small, and many of these were decorated with coloured glass windows. Even today, where these old windows have been preserved, the visitor must take pleasure in the supernatural–looking splendour of the coloured lights. Self–portraits of artists are very rare during the Middle Ages, because people considered artists as ordinary handicraft workers. Artists didn't think of signing their work any more than joiners, smiths or tailors thought of putting their names on things they made. So Gerlachus' picture is a notable exception.

4

4 In earlier times books were written by hand. They were often decorated with pictures which we call miniatures. In our next picture, which actually measures only three inches by two–and–a–half, we can see a woman artist painting her own portrait. With the help of the mirror in her left hand she is trying to trace her features very precisely. The book that contains this miniature is a collection of stories about famous men and women, among them the life of this painter Marcia. This new interest in the past, and in the personal experiences of individual people, is a sign that the Middle Ages are drawing to an end, for up to this point nearly all books had been concerned solely with religion.

The painter is wearing a long and elegant, soft, flowing dress, and she sits upon an ornamented chair. The picture she is working on is propped up on the back of a bench. Her equipment, which consists of an odd–shaped palette,

the brushes and the little bowls of paint, have been very neatly drawn. At that time a different brush was used for each colour. We can also see a shell, which is well suited for holding paint or oil. The restful, dark blue background of the painted portrait draws our attention away from the many small details. We know that in many artists' studios of the late Middle Ages the wife and daughters of the master–painter worked too. Doesn't the delicacy of this picture suggest that it was a woman's hand that painted it?

About fifty years after the making of this book with the picture of Marcia in it, Johannes Gutenberg invented printing, with individual pieces of type. In printed books there was no longer any room for hand–painted pictures.

5 At almost the same time as the little illustration of the woman artist the Italian sculptor Nanni di Banco carved these stone-

5

4 In earlier times books were written by hand. They were often decorated with pictures which we call miniatures. In our next picture, which actually measures only three inches by two-and-a-half, we can see a woman artist painting her own portrait. With the help of the mirror in her left hand she is trying to trace her features very precisely. The book that contains this miniature is a collection of stories about famous men and women, among them the life of this painter Marcia. This new interest in the past, and in the personal experiences of individual people, is a sign that the Middle Ages are drawing to an end, for up to this point nearly all books had been concerned solely with religion.

The painter is wearing a long and elegant, soft, flowing dress, and she sits upon an ornamented chair. The picture she is working on is propped up on the back of a bench. Her equipment, which consists of an odd-shaped palette, the brushes and the little bowls of paint, have been very neatly drawn. At that time a different brush was used for each colour. We can also see a shell, which is well suited for holding paint or oil. The restful, dark blue background of the painted portrait draws our attention away from the many small details. We know that in many artists' studios of the late Middle Ages the wife and daughters of the master-painter worked too. Doesn't the delicacy of this picture suggest that it was a woman's hand that painted it?

About fifty years after the making of this book with the picture of Marcia in it, Johannes Gutenberg invented printing, with individual pieces of type. In printed books there was no longer any room for hand-painted pictures.

5 At almost the same time as the little illustration of the woman artist the Italian sculptor Nanni di Banco carved these stone-

5

13

6

masons at work, as a decoration for the guild-hall in Florence. There is no feeling of delicacy or prettiness here; in fact we get a good idea of what heavy physical work stonemasons had to do.

On the left a wall is being built with stone blocks. Important tools, a setsquare and a plumb–line, are hanging up. Next to them a mason is picking up a drill to work on the artfully twisted column which is lying on trestles in front of him. The third artist has a thick beard. He is measuring up a capital with the setsquare. Perhaps it is intended to go on the top of the column. The last stonemason is carving a fat little cherub. The figures, you can see, are half–raised from the background. This kind of sculpture is called *relief.* Various decorative devices, and the clearly–depicted clothing of the craftsmen, complete this glimpse into a stonemasons' workshop during the late Middle Ages.

6 The next picture is a miniature of brick-layers and stonemasons working on the building of churches and convents. It dates from 1460, about fifty years after Nanni di Banco's sculpture. There are several different building sites, and on them we can see every kind of job being done, from the man mixing mortar in the foreground to the roofing worker in the distance. If you study all these details you will see that exactly the same work is still carried out today, on smaller building sites,

as was done five hundred years ago. But what is especially remarkable here is the way the artist has managed to include such a multitude of things in such a small surface area, without them getting in each others' way. The richly curling tendrils in the frame are meant to make the picture stand out, and give it a really sumptuous appearance.

7 In the Middle Ages men believed that the stars influenced their lives. The seven planets, they thought, had an especially strong influence on the followers of certain profes-sions. Such men were known as 'children' of the planets. This miniature shows the children of the planet Mercury. They are at work in small houses whose front walls have been taken away so that we can see inside. In the upper left-hand corner a scribe is sitting at his lectern. Below him are two watchmakers, and at the bottom is an armourer, whose trade was making weapons. Mercury was also thought to be important for innkeepers, and the artist has shown this by drawing a kitchen range and dining men in the centre of the picture. The right-hand row begins at the top with a painter in front of an opened out little gilded, winged altar. Next comes a sculptor, working on a statue with his hammer and chisel. Lastly comes an organ–maker. Thanks to the super-stitious beliefs of the past, we have here a particularly nice representation of artists and craftsmen at work.

7

8 The relief carving from an altar represents Saint Luke painting the Madonna. Saint Luke served as the patron saint of artists in the Middle Ages, because, according to legend, he painted Mary during her lifetime. A little bull lies beneath his chair: it is his evangelist's symbol. Mary and the painter are sitting opposite each other. The easel is set up between them. It consists of a board with holes in, so that the artist can fix pegs in it to fasten pictures at different heights. Mary is busy with the housework. She is sewing a shirt which is stretched out on a tailor's dummy. The baby Jesus is playing at her feet. The carver has placed great importance on working out the folds in her flowing garments as richly as possible. He has also lavished extraordinary care on the Madonna's beautiful, long curling hair. The whole scene is enclosed within a vaulted room, which, with all its cupboards and furniture, makes a really domestic and cosy impression.

16

9 Just as Saint Luke was considered the patron saint of painters, Saint Elijah was revered by smiths and goldsmiths. This late Gothic engraving depicts him, dressed in bishop's robes, as a master goldsmith in his workshop. He is shaping the upper part of a goblet or chalice on the anvil. For the first time we are shown here a real workshop. On the left the apprentice is using pliers to pull wire through a series of holes in a metal plate, to make it thinner. Behind him stands a furnace with bellows. The workbench stands in the right–hand half of the picture. It has a raised rim to stop even the tiniest bits of the costly precious metal from falling off. The pieces of leather spread under the benches have the same

purpose. The young man with the cap is a journeyman, who is choosing jewels for decorating the chalice. Next to him a boy is making patterns on his piece of work with a metal stamp. This is called embossing. All kinds of tools are lying on the bench. More equipment, such as tongs, hammer and files hangs tidily in the cupboard. A bowl of flowers stands by the open window, and a balance for weighing gold hangs from the window frame. Domestic animals are romping around the studio. Although Saint Elijah has been placed in the centre, he is not in fact the most significant part of the picture. The artist seems more interested in showing us the activity in the workshop, with its many fascinating details.

When rich men and nobles were patrons of the arts

10 As we saw in the picture of the Greek vase painter, people for a long time had loved to have beautiful crockery, either for use or just for ornament. The decorating of vases, plates and bowls is actually one of the oldest of all arts, and is still carried on today, all over the world. Our plate comes from Italy, and was made over 450 years ago. The painter has drawn himself in its centre, painting

10

yet another plate. Two visitors to the studio are watching him as he works. The man in particular is following the progress of the work most attentively, and is bending curiously forward. Has he perhaps specially ordered the plate, for his wife, or his bride?

It is quite surprising to see the artist so well dressed for his work. He has put just a cloth over his knees to protect himself from paint drips. Perhaps the clothes are meant to demonstrate that he is not an ordinary handworker, but a respectable citizen. Next to him on a small table stand the pots of colour that he needs for this painting: blue, yellow, orange, green, red and violet. This kind of Italian enamelled pottery is known as *majolika*. The plate was first fired, then painted, then glazed and finally fired again. That is how magnificently decorated pottery was produced about 500 years ago, and some can still be found in museums today, for us to appreciate. This particular plate is in the Victoria and Albert Museum, London.

11 We saw from our very first picture, the scene with Egyptian artists in a tomb, that wall painting (or mural painting) has a long and important history. A book miniature from about the same time as the majolika plate gives us a picture of a wall painter decorating a small banqueting hall. He is sitting on a bench on top of a high table, which is set up right against the wall. His paints and equipment are lying beside him. A few aldermen have come to look at the unfinished paintings. Perhaps one of them is the master painter, and he is interpreting his journeyman's work to his patrons. On the far wall is a folded-up table, with a window next to it. Above it a sort of picture

rail runs round the room. The flat surface above it, right up to the ceiling, is for painting. The standing figures represent the seasons of the year: on the left a girl depicts Summer, while Autumn and Winter are on the far wall. Between them, painted very small, are the coats of arms of Lithuania and Poland, being supported by so-called 'wild men'. These were spirits of the forest, who played an important part in the folklore of the Middle Ages. Inscriptions unfurled on scrolls complete the paintings. The picture is bordered around the top with a complex arrangement of ornamental leaves. At the bottom is the coat of arms of the painter's guild, with three shields.

What can be the significance of that Turk, whom the artist is just painting on the wall? A glance at history will give us the answer. In the fourteenth century the Turks began prolonged campaigns of conquest. In 1453 they captured Constantinople, the capital of the Byzantine Empire. The whole of Europe shook before their armies, and there are a lot of references to Turks in the art of the time. The intention must have been to give a continual reminder of the danger that threatened.

12 Albrecht Dürer, the most important German artist in the period after the end of the Middle Ages, left not only a huge number of beautiful paintings and drawings, but also several books on painting, whose aim was to share his discoveries with others. For apprentices to the craft of painting, and for his pupils, he wrote a book with the beautiful title: *The Feast of the Painter's Boy,* in which he laid down the basic rules of painting and drawing. In 1525 he published his book *The Teaching of Measurement.* The woodcut of an artist and a

Vnd so em Junger   arblcunce zo zal
Cet wandern ij   per yn ander Cant

12

sitting man is taken from it. Dürer is here demonstrating how, with the aid of a framed glass screen, you can draw all manner of three–dimensional shapes onto a flat surface. It is essential for this that the artist's eye should always remain at the same point, and this is achieved by making him look through a pierced plate on the top of a rigid stick.

Artists at this time were looking for ways to make their pictures ever truer to life and nature: they sought to create an impression of distance, and to suggest that objects in a picture had depth. They invented a method of doing this which we call perspective. This discovery, to which Dürer contributed a great deal, was a remarkable scientific achievement, of great importance for art in the following centuries.

Dürer realized that human understanding cannot penetrate and comprehend everything at once, but he never wished to give up the search for truth. He left these encouraging words for his readers: 'Because we may not come to perfect truth, should we then altogether give up our learning? We do reject such brutish thoughts.'

13 The woodcut by Erhard Schön, a pupil of Dürer's, gives us a chance to watch a wood carver at work. He has fastened his block to trestles with iron clamps, and is at present still carving the figure roughly into shape, for which he uses an axe. Already we can see the outline of the figure, and the head is developed somewhat farther. The tools lying on the floor are particularly interesting. Nearest the bottom is a yardstick, above it a setsquare. They are both used for taking measurements, as we have already seen with the Italian stonemasons. With the compasses the carver transfers individual measurements, either from the model or within his carved figure. The various shaped axes are for the rough shaping of the baulk of timber. There is a plane for smoothing flat surfaces, while for the detailed work there are chisels, which are struck with the mallet.

The elegantly dressed lady is motioning towards the group on the right, where the model for the statue seems to be being forcibly held there by the other two men. Behind them a fence of plaited branches forms a background to the scene. Many woodcarvings of medieval or later times are such finely detailed pieces of work that it can be hard to imagine that they were all worked out of a rough block like the one in the picture. But in this woodcut we have it most emphatically illustrated for us, and we recognize how difficult such work was.

Why does the model look so anxious to get away? The woodcut is a reference to a German proverb: 'Some bridegrooms need the rough edges knocking off them, before they become good husbands.'

13

14

14 In the artist's studio painted by Jan Mienze Molenaer there are great fun-and-games going on. In the foreground a dwarf is dancing with his little dog, to the music of the lyre that the old man is playing. The tankard falling down with a crash has fetched a painter out of the next room. He is standing behind the chair with the cape on it, holding his palette and mahlstick, and wanting to know what is going on. The maid seems to be warning them with her finger not to get carried away. The

picture on the easel shows the same scene again, but in a different arrangement. The canvas has laces round it to stretch it onto the oversized frame. In those days the modern type of wedged stretcher-frame hadn't been thought of, so artists managed in this way. The painter of this picture within a picture, who is busy mixing his paints, laughs at the dancers over his shoulder. Behind the old musician you can see a map of the world on the wall. It is a reminder that at this time the

24

Dutch sailed the oceans with their ships, carrying on a flourishing trade as far away as India, and earning great wealth.

But who are these dancing music–makers? They are wandering tumblers, who move on from village to village and live on alms which the onlookers give them in return for entertainment. People were happy when such entertainers came by, but didn't want too much to do with them, because they led disorderly lives and didn't have proper jobs. Even the respectable painter must have taken pleasure in such people, to want to paint them. Of course the tumblers couldn't buy the picture from him, but somebody else might think it valuable enough to give money for it and hang it in his home.

15 The scene in a studio was painted by Michiel Sweerts, who was a seventeenth century Dutch painter. At this time you would have found artists' studios looking like this

15

almost anywhere in Europe. On the left a student is sitting with his drawing board, studying the stone figure of a man standing in the middle of the room. A second student can be seen in the background. On the right is a heap of plaster casts of Greek and Roman statuary, lying untidily on top of each other. People took the art of these ancient civilizations as a model of beauty, and casts like this were used for copying, especially while you were still learning to draw. On the left, in the background, another painter is sitting at his easel. But he seems to be working from a living model, not copying a statue. Visitors stand to one side, watching the activity in the studio and perhaps looking out for a picture to buy. The man on the right is grinding substances to make paints, for at that time the artist had to prepare his own colours, or employ someone to do it for him. It was only much later that artists' paints began to be made in factories. The high window in the studio provided a special kind of light. A light coming from high up on one side was especially well-suited for drawing the human body. Often additional curtains were hung up, to get the best possible lighting conditions for a particular model.

16 'Las Meninas', The Maids of Honour' is the title of a big picture which the Spanish court painter Diego Velazquez painted in 1656. In the centre of the scene stands the five-year-old Princess Margarita Maria. By this time Spain had already lost its position as a world power, but the king's court was still dominated by strict ceremony. From her early childhood a princess was the centre of an elaborate routine. She had ladies in waiting and servants at her disposal, and, as we can see from the picture, even a glass of water had to be offered to her on a gold tray, by a kneeling attendant. The rules about court dress obliged this little princess to wear the shapeless hooped dress, which prevented any sort of childish movement.

On the right stands a fat, ugly little woman in expensive clothes. She belongs to the troupe of dwarfs who were kept at the court to provide entertainment. They had to amuse the elegant people there, and were meant to make the normal-sized members of the royal household look finer and more perfect, in the eyes of guests, than they really were.

On the left you can see the back of a huge canvas, and behind it stands the painter himself, looking right out of the picture at us. In fact he is looking at the little princess's parents, King Philip IV and his wife Marianne; it is their portrait he is painting. The proof of that can be glimpsed in the mirror on the far wall of this room in the palace at Madrid: there we can just catch sight of the royal couple. The parents have had their little daughter and her attendants brought along, to help pass the time, and Velazquez has taken the whole fascinating scene and made a painting of it. It is wonderful how he bathes the figures in light, and picks out with it the beauty of the different costly fabrics.

17 Artists have to learn their jobs, like everybody else. Nowadays you would probably go to college, but in earlier times you would have gone to study with an established painter who gave lessons. Even after their proper education, young artists often try to learn more by travelling to visit other well–known artists, or even by working with them for a while in their studios. Our picture shows just such a lesson. It happened over 200 years ago in London. Unfortunately we know the names of only two of the people in it. On the far left is Benjamin West. He is making suggestions about his work to Matthew Pratt, who is also, in fact, the painter of this whole picture. It is called 'The American School'. Young American artists have come to London to study with their experienced colleague West. They are all wearing the clothes of that period: a long coat, worn over a jacket, knee–breeches, and tight stockings with buckle shoes. The painting master is wearing a three–cornered hat. The others are waiting their turn patiently, while Pratt listens attentively to what West is saying. The painter on the right has only just begun his picture; apart from the drapery in one corner of it there is nothing to be seen.

18 In the etching by Daniel Chodowiecki, done in 1771, the family home has been turned into a studio. The artist made this picture to send to his mother from Berlin. He had left home twenty–eight years before and had not seen her since. He wanted to show her as accurately as possible how he and his family lived, and so he drew in all the details as exactly as he could. He himself is sitting in the background at the window, working at a little picture, which is probably the portrait of his eldest daughter. He keeps looking at her carefully over the top of his glasses. The five children have gathered round the table with their mother. On the left Jeanette is looking at a big book with pictures, while her sister standing next to her enjoys the caresses of her mother. Disappearing in the much–too–big armchair we catch a glimpse of the one–year–old youngest child of the family. The four–year–old son would like to see the horse that his eldest brother is drawing, but he can hardly reach over the edge of the table.

18

The far wall of the room is covered in pictures. It was then quite usual to hang pictures close to each other and one above the other. Chodowiecki had a big art collection, and he also made some money dealing in paintings. The figures on the side table were part of this collection, and so were about 10,000 drawings, which were kept in files. The group of people stands out clearly from the dark surroundings. The whole scene radiates peace and contentment. We can feel how much pleasure the artist took in his family, and also his pride in the modest wealth that he had earned for them. Nothing has been dressed up to look better than it is: the chairs don't match each other, the table cloth is not straight, the curtain at the window has been pushed back and the doll carelessly thrown down. It all indicates the artist and engraver's middle class, matter-of-fact feeling for realism.

19 The next picture shows us a pair of porcelain figures: the portraitist and his model. The secret of making oriental porcelain was discovered in 1709 by Johann Friedrich Böttger, who was an alchemist and chemist from Dresden in Germany. Shortly afterwards the first European porcelain factory was set up. It was the business at Meissen, which is still flourishing today. They produced magnificent dinner-services there, often with hundreds of different pieces. At the same time their porcelain sculptors made some wonderful pieces of work. They produced figures or groups which were from four to twelve inches tall, representing animals, comedians, Chinamen, Turks, the four quarters of the world as they then knew it, the seasons, and different occupations. They were made to be set on festive banqueting tables in royal palaces, along with the candlesticks and the crockery. These eighteenth century porcelain models were small works of art, and straightaway became known all over the world. Their creators were famous artists, like Johann Joachim Kändler of Meissen.

Of course, artists are included among the models that represent different occupations: there are singers, musicians, dancers, sculptors and painters. The porcelain group in our picture was made in Vienna at about the same time as Daniel Chodowiecki in Berlin was drawing his family. The material is not glazed, and therefore has a flat, marble-like sheen. The delicate colouring looks as though it were done with pastel crayons. The painter, wearing a blue coat lined with yellow silk, is sitting comfortably at his easel, one leg crossed over the other, and using a red chalk fixed in something very like a penholder. He has other coloured pencils in his left hand as well as his palette, for he is not just going to draw his model, but paint her too. The young lady is dressed very elegantly, in the latest style. Her hair is also done in the fashionable way. She wants to look especially beautiful, and is taking great care to sit up very straight; she looks rather affected. But the painter is most interested in her features, and is studying her face closely. The sculptor of this group, Anton Grassi, has shown us, with light humour, a piece of the artist's day-to-day life from almost two centuries ago.

Artists in the age
of the Industrial Revolution

20 The painter Caspar David Friedrich stands bent over in front of the still-unfinished picture on his easel. He lived about two hundred years ago. His friend Georg Friedrich Kersting painted this picture of him in his studio at Dresden. We are looking into a bare room. The artist is holding his palette and a long mahlstick, which serves as a prop and support for his hand when he is working on finely-detailed parts of the canvas.

Caspar David Friedrich was above all a landscape painter. It is rather surprising to find him here, and not painting his picture out of doors in the country. We know, from letters and from friends' accounts of him, that he used to spend a lot of time walking in the countryside, and he also made drawings there. But he painted his pictures, which are carried out in fine detail, back at home in his studio. Another painter, Bernd von Kügelgen, later recorded memories of this studio, which he had seen when he was a child. 'Friedrich's studio was absolutely empty ... There was nothing in it apart from the easel, a chair and a table, over

which there hung as the only piece of mural decoration a setsquare, although nobody could ever understand how it came to achieve that particular distinction. Even such well-entitled things as paint-boxes, bottles of oil and painting rags had been banished to the next room, because Friedrich believed that all extraneous objects deeply disturbed the world inside the picture.'

So the artist had, from the moment he began the painting, a definite idea of how he wanted his picture to be. Nothing in the room should be allowed to disturb him. Friedrich's conviction was that the landscape painter's job was not simply to copy whatever bits of the countryside caught his fancy. With his pictures he was trying much more to awake special moods in the people who looked at them: the longing for distance and far-awayness, sorrow for days gone by, an awareness of the changing times of day and the seasons of the year, and a feeling of the unendingness of the world. He may have stood for hours in front of his painting, as Kersting portrayed him; silently pondering, and considering how to re-awaken in his picture the things he had experienced during his wanderings in the countryside.

21 Four young artists have left their studios and gone on a walking holiday. We can see from their weatherproof clothing, the large bags, the rucksack, the walking sticks and the umbrella that they expect to cover a fair distance. They want to study for themselves the different faces of the countryside, from towering mountains to wide spreading plains. One of them has sat down on a portable folding stool to draw. The drawing–board is fitted with a ring, through which a prop is pushed. The big umbrella has a metal point on the end, for anchoring it firmly in the ground. In this way the artists can work in all weathers, protected from rain and sun.

A period of travelling used to be part of the rounding–off of many handcraftsmen's education, painters included. They often covered great distances on foot or on horseback. We have the example of Albrecht Dürer, whose journeys to Italy, Holland and within Germany we can follow exactly by the drawings and watercolours that he made on the way. In the nineteenth century studies done in the open air were the essential basis of many artists' work. At first, however, the finished pictures were not done out of doors. The artist made drawings or sometimes water–colour sketches on paper, and these served him as memory aids when painting the actual picture on a wooden panel or on canvas, back in the studio.

22 At first sight this picture looks quite extraordinary. To understand it we must go back to the times in which it was made. In Europe in the first half of the nineteenth century young artists in fine art colleges were still learning to draw and paint almost entirely from plaster casts and other models. Nature was disapproved of as a source of inspiration, because it was considered imperfect. Many people still held that artists should only paint very important things, such as historical or religious events and characters. The stress

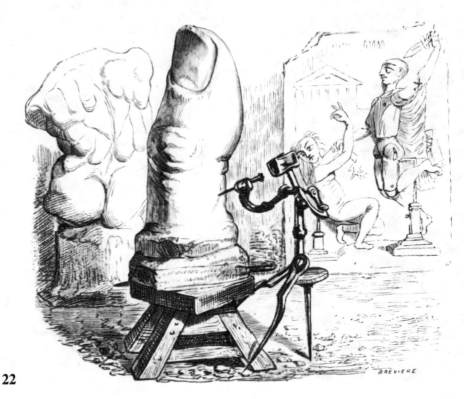

22

should be laid on majestic, heroic, larger–than–life themes, and everything should be made to look pleasing to the eye. Greek, Roman, and Italian art was taken as the great example of beauty, and it was constantly studied and imitated. Artists who worked purely from nature were not taken very seriously.

A Frenchman called Grandville made fun of this attitude in a woodcut called 'The Finger of God: a prodigious work'. A little awkward mechanical figure is working with his hammer–shaped head at a huge thumb. Grandville's intention here was to pour scorn on the artists of his day who, without using their heads, made lifeless copies of the works of art of past ages. They produced things which indeed looked monumental enough, but were in reality empty and worthless. On the right a woman is being attacked by an artist's lay figure wielding a knife. In those days dummies were much used in colleges and studios in place of living models. Grandville is suggesting how dangerous it can be when these lifeless aids become too powerful: they can threaten life itself, by destroying the artist's essential links with nature and with men. Grandville's wood–engraving is not merely funny and witty, but an effective attack on the wrong ideas and methods of certain artists, who had got too far away from reality.

23 One is inclined to take this impression of an artist's studio for the product of an over–active imagination. Yet it really was the workplace of the once–celebrated Austrian painter Hans Makart. Makart's pictures, usually huge things, resembled his studio, overloaded and so chock–full of detail that among them one can only pick out the really important things with great difficulty. At that time, lots of people went in for such ostentation. They bought up expensive things from all over the place, just to show off how rich they were. Nowadays we would find such an accumulation of objects in bad taste, and it is hard for us to imagine how an artist could ever work in such an atmosphere.

What a contrast to the plain, workmanlike studio of Caspar David Friedrich only fifty years earlier.

24 About one hundred years ago the Frenchman Edouard Manet painted his friend Claude Monet at work in his floating studio. We can see not only the people, the river and the landscape, but also actually feel the glaring sun, and the air shimmering in the heat.

Manet and Monet belonged to the Impressionists, as they were called. This was a group of artists who painted their pictures completely out of doors, because they thought that this was the only way to get an accurate impression of what one really sees and feels in the open air. Hence their name. They wanted to paint the real impressions made by nature: for instance, the transformations in the landscape caused by the changing light at different times of day, or during different seasons or different kinds of weather. For this reason they set up their studios entirely out of doors. They had to work very quickly, too, because lighting and weather often change very suddenly. The pictures which resulted from this were much brighter. New shades of colours appeared, so that even shadows looked not just dark, but coloured.

Working so quickly had the additional result that it was impossible to take great care and put in every single detail. But this doesn't mean they were careless; this was how the Impressionists wanted to paint. Of course, we must look at these pictures in a different way from the sort of picture where all the objects are drawn in detail, with clear outlines. There we can go up near to them and look at everything closely. With impressionist paintings, on the other hand, we must stand farther away and use our powers of imagination to complete the picture, or add a great deal to what is actually drawn in it.

The Impressionists, with their magnificently colourful paintings, discovered beautiful aspects of the world that until then had remained unnoticed.

A look into artists' studios in modern times

25 Marc Chagall, who was Russian by birth, was twenty–four years old as he stood at his easel in Paris and painted this self–portrait. He had in fact attended an art college in his home country, but it wasn't until he travelled to France to study that he found out how to give full expression to his talent. Many artists who were later to be famous, like Braque, Picasso and others, were at that time living in Paris, and searching for new ways to develop painting. This self–portrait of the young Chagall shows what a strong effect the new impressions of life in Paris had made on him. He is sitting in a bare room, through the window of which the Eiffel tower, the engineering marvel built just twenty years before, can be seen. On the easel stands a picture, which actually has nothing at all to do with Paris. Chagall liked to express in his paintings his longing for his far–off Russian homeland. On the canvas we can make out a Russian church, a red cow drinking out of a barrel, and a farmer with a bucket. Similar things appear in a cloud in the top right–hand corner.

Artists for hundreds of years had devoted all their skill to making pictures as true to life as possible. Now, at the beginning of this century, many of them began to re–fashion and change things to suit their own wishes and ideas. The painters known as cubists, for instance, based their pictures on geometrical forms. Chagall at the time was an admirer of theirs, and this explains the unusual shapes used here in the painter's face and body. He thought he could express his meaning better in this way than with an ordinary, realistic picture.

Of course Chagall knew that hands have five, not seven fingers. Perhaps by playing with the truth like this the idea was to bring us into the same fantasy–like mood in which he then found himself. He was one of many children in a very poor family. Mustn't it have seemed quite fantastic to him, to find himself fulfilling his hopes and dreams in the great city of Paris?

26 So far most of the pictures have shown an artist's studio, and described in detail this room, large or small, where the artist works, alone or with others. In 1932 Otto Dix did a painting which shows us another artist at work, his friend Willy Kriegel. We can't see anything of the size or appearance of the studio: the picture is taken up by the as yet unfinished painting on the easel, on which the artist is hard at work. It is a portrait of his wife. The first processes have been completed: the canvas has been primed and the basic features of the portrait outlined with the first strokes of the brush. Details are not yet to be seen. At the moment the artist, drawing more than painting with a fine–pointed brush, is working on the folds of the dress, putting in bright highlights with his oil paints. Thus with great care another layer of the painting is added. Before its completion further such layers will be painted, one on top of the other. They don't hide the colours beneath them, but let them shine through. The painter begins with the darkest shades, and then puts the lighter colours over, finishing his work with the lightest colour and then the varnish. In this way the colours take on lightness and depth. This technique was called *lasur* in German, which means glazing.

It demanded great care and concentration from the painter; he couldn't afford to let his attention wander. Otto Dix's painting is two–thirds taken up by the unfinished picture of the woman. In the lower third we can see the artist Kriegel. He is totally buried in his work and is holding the canvas steady on the easel to give him more control over the brush. He can depend on his memory now, and doesn't need the model to work from. Looking at this picture you should be able to feel right away the tension of the artist as he works. Thus anything happening round about, which could distract you, has been left out.

27 The painter Theodor Rosenhauer made a striking picture of an artist in his studio. He is sitting idly, leaning over the table with his head in his hands. A letter is lying in front of him. Two pictures are lying with their faces to the wall. They look as if they have just been taken down. Clothes are hanging untidily over the back of the chair and on the bed. The easel leans unused against the wall.

This picture was painted in 1935 in Germany. Two years before, the Nazis had come to power. Many German artists left their country then, partly because they were afraid of being

26

persecuted for their political views, and partly because they foresaw the evil times that were coming. Some artists were arrested, and others committed suicide. Many famous painters, actors and writers were prevented from working, because they refused to support Hitler through their art.

We don't know what the letter on the table says. Perhaps it is his call–up to the army, or perhaps it tells him that he must give up his work, or contains some other bad news. We can sense very clearly the artist's despair. Somehow the empty walls make us share in the feeling of numb shock that has come over him. He sits lost and small in the middle of the room, and the atmosphere seems charged with tension. In this way, without making any direct reference to the events of the time, the picture becomes a reflection of how life in Germany was, during these terrible times.

28 While the Soviet artist Korshev was on a visit to France to study in Paris, he saw there a painter working with coloured chalks on the pavement. Did he wish to display his skill to as many people as possible, to people who would otherwise never go to museums or art galleries? The cap with coins in it tells us the real reason: the painter is demonstrating his skill to the passers–by in the hope that they will give him money. He has become a beggar. The sad–faced woman leaning against the tree is his wife. You might think that this is a case of a not–very–gifted artist not being able to sell his paintings because they were not good enough. But many examples from the history of art tell us otherwise. There have been impor-

tant artists who had to suffer hunger and poverty during their lifetimes. Only later, often after their deaths, the prices for their paintings began to rise. In some cases people simply didn't appreciate what the artist was trying to show them. In many other cases however the prices were purposely kept low by art dealers, so that they could pick a favourable time to sell their pictures for the highest possible profit.

This big picture by Korshev makes its impression especially by its composition. We are looking down on the scene from above, and feel as if we ourselves were passers–by. In this way the degrading position of the painter is made very clear. The picture levels accusations against the sort of system that obliges an artist to set up his studio in the dust of the street, and ask for charitable donations.

29 The Frenchman Daguerre discovered the principle of photography in 1838. The process was steadily improved on, until at about the end of the nineteenth century came the instantaneous exposure, and a few years later the invention of moving pictures. Thus it became possible to record the making of a work of art much more directly than had previously been the case. So far we have seen pictures of artists at work from earliest times. They show clearly the tools of painters, sculptors and craftsmen, and also their studios, and the people with whom they worked. In this century it became possible to study even more closely that perpetually exciting process by which works of art are created. Thanks to photography and film, we can see the successive changes that a piece of work undergoes from its beginning to its completion. Photographic documentation exists of all the leading figures in the fine arts during this century, and there are even moving films of some. They follow the growth of a work of art so that the watcher can experience it for himself. Such films exist of Pablo Picasso, Lovis Corinth, Henri Matisse, Kaethe Kollwitz, and many other artists.

Our photo shows us one of the most important European sculptors of modern times, the Englishman Henry Moore, who was born in 1898. He is working on a wood sculpture. Moore has brought sculpture back to simple

29

30

shapes. At the same time the main themes of his extensive output of work show that he has never abandoned the connection with the human form. The 'mother and child' subjects, the sitting and above all the reclining female figures, who lie back supported on their elbows, occur repeatedly in his work from 1929 onward, and are generally his greatest achievements. Here he is busy on one of his seated or reclining figures. He works at the block of wood with a hammer and chisel, chipping it away until it takes on the final shape of the design, and finally smoothing the surface with successively finer tools.

30 The Mexican painter and architect Juan O'Gorman, who designed the huge mosaic on the library building of the University of Mexico City, also produced a special kind of portrait of himself at work. The painter has drawn himself no less than four times: once standing, once sitting down and seen from behind, once as a painted portrait, and once reflected in the mirror on the easel. Finally the painter's hand holding a brush appears from the bottom edge of the picture. He probably wished to present himself as a many-sided character, but here, as in certain other details, we are driven back on supposition. The Sun and the Moon hang like lamps in a blue sky; a winged imp sits on his shoulder, whispering something in his ear; a frog holds a ticket in its mouth; the same dove appears three times, and it too has a paper in its beak. The artist's name and the date of the picture are written on the Mexican flag which hangs in the top right-hand corner. The standing figure is holding the design for the whole picture in his right hand; you can see the ruler and compass lines on it. The imp's geometrical halo, the setsquare, the tee-square and the blueprints hint at the painter's other profession as an architect. Apparently he is keen on sport too; how else are we to explain the tennis racket? O'Gorman wanted not simply to show us what he looked like with his self-portrait, but has given the person who sees his picture something to think about too, something which cannot be made out entirely, or expressed in the form of words.

31 The Dresden graphic artist and painter Bernhard Kretschmar, the son of a shoemaker, born in Döbeln in 1889, lived a childhood of extreme poverty. He became a house decorator before he went to art school in Dresden in 1909. His prolific production, over a period of sixty years, includes oil paintings, water colours, drawings, and etchings. The hardships of his early life had a deep influence on his career as an artist. He wanted to show the life led by people like himself and reveal the causes of the poverty they lived in, at the same time reminding the viewer that life could have a better side. But if life was to be made better, the way of life in the passing imperial Germany and in the successor Weimar Republic had to undergo a change, and not the change brought about by the Nazis either. And thus Bernhard Kretschmar became an important social–critical artist, revealing the hauteur of the owning classes and their contempt for his kind of people, the have–nots of society.

Landscapes also fascinated him, and his work after the end of the Second World War includes many landscapes; bright, brilliant colours, with unfathomable blue skies; white clouds, often tinged pink, scudding across them. The painter's eye sweeps across the scene and captures a peaceful, happy landscape, in a homeland that people are changing for the better.

Just such a picture is his 'Fire in summer', painted in 1953. The painter has put up a portable easel on a strip of meadowland near a coppice. Over the edge of the grassland we see a view of fields of ripe corn. Under the painter's hands the harmonious atmosphere of the late summer is growing up on the canvas. But a dark, brown–and–green–and–black column of smoke is rising from a far–off field. A fire has broken out. The spell of the peaceful scene is broken.

Since the time of the French Impressionists one hundred years ago, who went outdoors to paint nature direct, outdoor painting has again become rare, and the artists have returned to their indoor studios. Bernhard Kretschmar combines the best of both worlds in his pictures: they are light and colourful like those of the Impressionists without sacrificing any clarity. Again and again they reveal the beauty of nature around us.

31

32 To finish with let us look at a painting by Pablo Picasso. He was born in Spain, but has lived since the beginning of the century in France. He has often drawn artists and painters with their models, almost always in series, in a sequence of several pictures or drawings. The theme is always the full–grown artist practising his profession. Once, however, in 1923, he painted his four–year–old son Paolo drawing a picture. Unselfconsciously, the little boy sits at a table and scribbles on the paper in front of him. With an unpractised hand he makes lines and circles, creating his own world. He isn't trying to copy the things around him or what he sees directly in front of him. Instead he is trying to draw what he sees in his imagination. Not until he is older will he set himself to drawing his gentle playmate, the good–natured fat pug that he certainly loves very dearly.

The world itself can be embraced:
we can take possession of it with no more than a pencil, pen or paintbrush.
We can recognize what is beautiful in it,
and understand what is ugly and evil.
Is that something you have ever tried for yourself?

An explanation of some of the terms used in this book

Alchemist — Long before the beginnings of modern science men tried to solve the mysteries of nature. Alchemists devoted themselves to investigating the materials which make up the Earth, and in this way became the forerunners of present-day chemists and scientists. Their work was still mixed up with magic, however. For hundreds of years they tried to find a way of making gold from other substances. In this they were doomed to failure of course, but they did succeed, often quite accidentally, in making some important and useful discoveries, out of all their heating and mixing of different substances.

Architect and Architecture — When a new house is built, the builder needs a plan to work from, and this is drawn up by an architect. When he is designing a building an architect has to keep in mind what it will be used for, and also try to make it attractive both inside and out. To become an architect you have to study for some years. The art of building is called architecture. It covers the designing and erection of single buildings, groups of buildings and even whole towns. With so many buildings all around us the whole time, architecture has a strong influence on our entire lives.

Capital — This word comes from Latin, and means 'head'. It is the name we give to the carved piece of stone which sits on the top of a pillar or column. If you look at the capitals in churches you will sometimes find them decorated with skilful and imaginative carvings.

Carving — Sculpture in wood or ivory is usually called carving. The most famous English carver was Grinling Gibbons (1648—1721). Other great carvers were the Germans Michael Pacher (1430—1498) and Veit Stoss (1447—1542).

Ceramics — *Keramos* is the Greek word for pottery. By ceramics we mean objects that are made out of clay and then fired. We have to distinguish between rough ceramics, like fire bricks, roofing tiles and pipes, and fine ceramics like vases, plates, sculptures and decorative tiles.

Cubism — This is a type of painting which was important in the early years of this century. The cubist painters reduced objects to square, or sometimes cylindrical or round shapes. By splitting their subjects, even portraits of people, into lots of little shapes, the cubists could show many facets of them at the same time. It was a method, quite different from perspective, of giving a sort of three-dimensional effect on flat canvas. Later cubist paintings became more and more abstract until the subject can hardly be recognized at all. In these paintings it is just the shapes and colours that give the picture its impact. The cubist movement owed a great deal to Pablo Picasso and to George Braque.

Etching — Etching is one of the graphic arts. A metal plate is covered with lacquer, in which the artist scratches the design with a pointed tool. The finished plate is put in a bath of acid which eats away the exposed metal, leaving grooves. To print from the plate it is coated with printer's ink so that the ink soaks into the grooves. The surface is then wiped clear of ink and the plate put in a printing press. The ink held in the grooves is forced onto the paper. This type of printing, where the design is actually below the surface of the plate, is called intaglio. It is not like a woodcut or linocut, for instance, where it is the raised parts of the block that carry the ink and print the design.

Evangelists' Symbols — The four Evangelists, Matthew, Mark, Luke and John, were the men who wrote down the gospel of Christ, in books which became part of the New Testament. They were often represented by their emblems or symbols, which are: an angel (Matthew), a lion (Mark), a bull (Luke), and an eagle (John). The earliest pictures of the Evangelists that we have date from the fourth century.

Fascism in Germany — In 1933 Adolf Hitler, leader of the Nazi party (National Socialists), came to power in Germany. Hitler's promises to make Germany powerful and wealthy again won the votes of many Germans who disliked the results of having lost the First World War (1914/18). Many people had no jobs, and they were ready to give Hitler wide powers if he could improve living conditions. But Hitler used his power in evil ways. We can describe Germany under Hitler as a fascist state. All opposition was stamped out. Jews, communists, and anybody who opposed Hitler's ideas were persecuted and put in concentration camps; many of them were killed. Hitler's schemes to enlarge Germany ended in the Second World War. When Germany was defeated in 1945 he killed himself. Since the end of the war Germany has been divided into two countries.

Glaze — The glaze is the glassy surface on pottery, which is put on to close up the fine pores. This makes glazed pottery waterproof. Glazing also makes pottery more beautiful, adding shine, smoothness and colour to it.

Gothic — Gothic is the name we use for the type of architecture which flourished in the Middle Ages. We have seen that when people re–discovered the ancient civilizations of Greece and Rome they began to copy their art and also their architecture. When they looked back at the churches and cathedrals that had been built in the Middle Ages they condemned them as primitive works, and so they called them Gothic, after the Goths, a savage tribe which had once swept over Europe. For a long time we have recognized how beautiful our medieval churches really are, but the name Gothic has stuck. From simple beginnings Gothic architecture became increasingly decorated and technically advanced. Huge windows decorated with stained glass, tall ceilings of intricate stone vaulting, pinnacles, spires and beautiful stone sculptures all help to make a late Gothic cathedral tremendously impressive, even to our modern eyes. It is no wonder that such buildings took whole lifetimes to complete, by medieval builders working with simple tools.

Graphic arts — Graphic art is art intended for reproduction by printing. Nowadays photographic methods can be used to make a printing plate from any picture. Traditionally, however, the artist had to work directly on the wood or stone block, or the metal plate, which was to be used for printing the picture. These methods (which many artists still use) are called *autographic,* and include the wood or lino cut, wood engraving, lithography, copper engraving and etching.

Guilds — In medieval times the guilds were organizations of handcraftsmen in different trades. The guilds had strict rules, for example about the education of apprentices, the acceptance of new members, the quality of work; they also protected the rights of their members and settled disputes.

Lay figure — This is a jointed wooden doll, which can be dressed in different ways, and which an artist uses when he can't get a live model to pose for him. Used intelligently it can be a great help; but the artist should never try to manage without the study of real–life models.

Mahlstick — This is a long thin stick, usually with a little pad at the top, which an artist leans his painting hand on. It makes it easier to paint very fine details without touching and spoiling other still wet parts of the picture.

Majolika — This is the name for a special type of pottery, mostly crockery and vases, made in Italy between the fourteenth and eighteenth centuries. It can be recognized by the beautiful patterns and figures that were painted in the opaque, usually white glaze before the second firing. The name Majolika comes from Majorca, the Spanish island in whose ports the pottery was bought by traders.

Middle Ages — It is convenient to divide history into four rough sections: ancient history, the Dark Ages, the Middle Ages, and modern history. The Middle Ages covers roughly the period 1100—1500 A.D. In Europe Christianity and the Christian Church was then the strongest influence on men's thoughts and feelings, and most art in this period is concerned with religious scenes and figures. The Middle Ages were followed by the Renaissance, which led on to modern times.

Miniature — This word has two meanings. It is the name for very small paintings, usually portraits. They were so small they could be mounted in lockets, so that ladies might have pictures of their true loves to hang round their necks. Miniatures are also the small pictures used to decorate hand–written books.

Model — When an artist includes a human figure in his painting or drawing his model is the person he copies and works from. In sculpture the word can mean the fullscale clay or plaster model which a sculptor makes before starting work on his block of stone.

Museum — Museums are places where very valuable, rare and interesting things are kept and displayed. There are museums for all kinds of subjects: folklore, natural history, geology, fine arts, vintage cars and so on.

Murals — Murals are paintings on walls. There are two methods of mural painting: in the first the artist works with wet plaster, and this is very difficult because it must be done section by section. The colours are very clear, however, and don't fade easily. This is called fresco painting. The other method is to paint onto dry plaster. In this way fine details can be put in, but the paint doesn't stick to the wall so well, and the painting can be damaged more easily.

Palette — A painter uses his palette for mixing colours. Palettes can be various shapes, but are usually oval boards with a hole for the artist's thumb at one end.

Perspective — *Perspicere* is Latin and means 'to look through'. Perspective is a way of drawing which makes things in a flat picture look as if they are really solid and have depth. The artist manages this by drawing things that are farther away smaller than things in the foreground, and making lines converge in a particular way in the distance. There are precise rules to be followed in perspective drawing. The mathematical basis for these rules was worked out by the Italian architect Brunelleschi about six hundred years ago. The first painter to use them was the Italian painter Masaccio, in 1420—25.

Pharaoh — The pharaohs were the all-powerful rulers of ancient Egypt, who were worshipped as gods.

Planets — The planets are satellites that revolve round the Sun. They include Saturn, Mars, Jupiter, Venus and Mercury. There are at least three more, Uranus, Neptune and Pluto, but people in earlier times didn't know about them, because they can't be seen without very good telescopes. Men used to call the Sun and Moon planets too, when they thought that the Earth was the centre of the Universe and that all other heavenly bodies revolved round it. The planets were named after the Greek gods and represented their different characteristics. In ancient times and in the Middle Ages men thought that the stars had a powerful influence on their lives. Thus people who came under the influence of Mars were meant to be very warlike (Mars was the god of war) while those influenced by Mercury were meant to be ingenious and inventive. Many medieval books have pictures illustrating the relationships of the 'planet children' to their planets.

Plastic arts — The plastic arts include sculpture, carving, and other such works of art that are not flat but three-dimensional.

Portrait — A portrait is always a picture of some definite person. Portraits can be paintings, drawings, or sculptures.

Punch — A punch is a tool for stamping, and is made out of steel. It is held against the metal surface to be decorated, and when it is struck with a hammer the pattern is imprinted on the metal. Goldsmiths particularly use punches to decorate precious pieces of work. Bookbinders and gold-leaf-workers use them too.

Renaissance — This is a French word meaning rebirth. It is the name we give to the period when the culture and knowledge of the Greeks and Romans was re-discovered, after it had been forgotten for over a thousand years. The Renaissance began in Italy in about 1400, and spread to England rather later. At that time many Greek and Roman works of art were excavated and re-discovered. It was the wealthy city-dwellers and artists who were most excited by these new-found beauties. Here was the inspiration of an ancient art which was quite different from anything the Middle Ages had known. Men turned away from their old ideas about the world, and began to look afresh at nature and at mankind. They laid the foundations of the modern sciences. Artists created true-to-life and beautiful works, which are examples for us even today.

Sculptor — A sculptor is an artist who carves figures in stone. It is not easy work. The sculptor, just like the stone-mason, has to master the difficulties of working in stone. Above all, he has to have a very clear idea from the very beginning of how the figure should look, because although he can chip pieces off his block of stone, he can't put anything back. For this reason many sculptors make a model first, of plaster or clay, then take the measurements for the real statue from it. Some sculptors, however, begin straight away with the stone. The work of the sculptor is called sculpture, or the plastic arts. One of the greatest sculptors was the Italian Michelangelo Buonarroti. Sculpture is a very ancient art. Carved figures and models are among the very earliest remains left by human beings.

Sphinx — An imaginary beast with a lion's body and a human head, which was worshipped by some ancient peoples.

Vase — Vases are nowadays mostly used for putting flowers in, but in earlier times served various purposes, such as storing liquids, or for drinking, or just as ornaments. The ancient Greeks made particularly splendid vases, in all kinds of shapes and nearly always beautifully painted. They used two distinct styles: black designs on red pottery, and red designs on a black surface.

Wedged frame — Painters nowadays use a frame with wedges to stretch their canvas tight. It is made of four pieces of wood that slot together at the corners. Wedges are driven into these slots in each angle, so that the sides are forced outwards and the canvas is drawn tight.

Woodcuts and wood engraving — Woodcuts are made with a knife, while for wood engravings the artist uses a fine point. Pear wood is generally used, but sycamore, lime and cherry are also suitable. The artist cuts the surface of a block of wood so that the design is left standing up. These raised surfaces are inked with printer's ink, so that when the block is pressed on paper the design is printed.

Sources of Pictures

Copyright Edition Leipzig 1973
Lic. 600/22/72
All rights reserved. No part of this publication
may be reproduced, stored in a retrieval system,
or transmitted, in any form or by any means, electronic,
mechanical, photocopying, recording or otherwise,
without the prior permission of Edition Leipzig
Designer: Walter Schiller Altenburg
Printed in the German Democratic Republic
by VEB Offsetdruck Leipzig

The Artist
By John Bianchi

Bungalo Books

Written by John Bianchi
Illustrated by John Bianchi
Copyright 1993 by Bungalo Books

Canadian Cataloguing in Publication Data

Bianchi, John
   The Artist

ISBN 0-921285-29-9 (bound)   ISBN 0-921285-28-0 (pbk.)

1. Title.

PS8553.I26A78 1993   jC813'.54   C93-090379-X
PZ7.B43Ar 1993

Published in Canada by: Trade Distribution:
Bungalo Books   Firefly Books Ltd.
Box 129   250 Sparks Avenue
Newburgh, Ontario   Willowdale, Ontario
KOK 2S0   M2H 2S4

Co-published in U.S.A. by: Printed in Canada by:
Firefly Books (U.S.) Inc.   Friesen Printers
Ellicott Station   Altona, Manitoba
P.O. Box 1338
Buffalo, New York 14205

This book was created and published
without government grants or subsidies.

In memory of Jean Richard
1939 - 1991

and to Lupcia and Ian,
who provided the inspiration

Even when he was very young, Amelio loved to paint. Though his paintbox was small, his imagination was immense, and he would often work for hours painting remarkable pictures while dreaming of a life as a great artist.

When he grew older, Amelio loved to go to the park to study the famous artists of the day. He would often make notes and drawings in a small sketchbook that was with him wherever he went.

Sometimes, he would visit Henri Maltese, known for his legendary experiments with colour.

Other times, he would stop for a chat with Dame Emily van Borzoi, whose powerful landscapes were filled with magnificent light. And he would never miss a chance to watch Camille Briard, whose use of radical composition had turned the art world upside down.

Amelio could not wait to grow up and follow in the footsteps of his heroes. Someday, he, too, would be a painter of great landscapes.

But luck was not with Amelio. Times turned tough, and each member of the family had to help out.

"And what will you do?" asked Amelio's mother.

"I will paint faces in the little park by the Gorgonzola Bridge," said Amelio.

And that is exactly what he did. In fact, he became well known for the glorious rainbows he would paint on the cheeks of his young customers.

But this left no time for painting great landscapes.

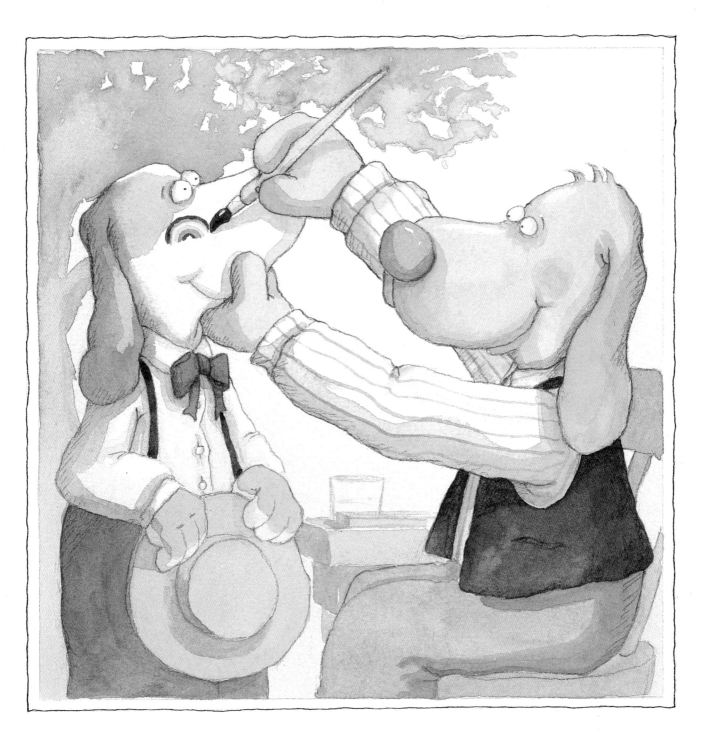

When he was older, Amelio decided to attend art school.

"And how will you pay for your education?" asked Amelio's father.

"I will sketch portraits of the ladies and gentlemen in the town square," replied Amelio.

And that is exactly what he did.

While he was at art school, Amelio fell in love with the beautiful Lemonjello.

"Will you marry me?" asked Amelio one day while they were dancing at the café.

"Of course!" replied Lemonjello.

"And how will you two support yourselves?" asked their parents when they had been told the news.

"I will create fashion designs for all the famous dress salons," said Lemonjello.

"And I will make posters for the town's opera house," replied Amelio.

Amelio and Lemonjello hoped to have a large family, and when the little ones arrived, Amelio took an extra job working nights at the Provolone Sign Company.

Now, the painting of great landscapes was nothing more than a distant memory that would sometimes visit Amelio while he was inscribing an especially ornate letter on one of his signs . . .

. . . or changing a diaper on one of his puppies.

Whenever the town needed an artist, Amelio was always there.

He designed packages for the Presto Pasta Company, fashioned greeting cards for the Mama Mia Stationery Store and sketched courtroom scenes for the town newspaper. He even helped a local architect design affordable houses.

And so went the artist's life. Happily distracted by the joys of his family and his work, Amelio had no chance to create great landscapes.

Only in his later years did Amelio finally find time to paint. On sunny days, he would visit the park to work on his landscapes . . . but would usually end up entertaining his many grandpups.

One day, when he was was quite old, Amelio fell gravely ill. A doctor was summoned, and his family gathered around him. All knew that Amelio was not long for this world. Some started to cry.

"Please," said Amelio, "do not cry for me. I have had a good, long life and have been able to watch you all grow up. I only wish I had had more time to spend with the beautiful Lemonjello and maybe a few more moments to paint pictures of this wonderful land."

The old artist died that night and was immediately escorted to heaven by an angel. After a hot bath and a chocolate cappuccino, Amelio was given a new robe, a fresh set of wings and a halo. Then he was brought before God.

"My staff and I have watched your life with much interest," said God. "And since you have led an honest and kindly life and have always cared for your family, we have decided to grant you a permanent place in heaven.

"Now, the first thing you'll need is a job – we like to keep our new angels as busy as possible. Let's see . . ."

God started reading through his job file.

"We have openings for a face painter: 'must have previous experience.' A portrait artist: 'please show samples of recent work.' And a sign painter: 'must be able to spell big words.'

"You may have your choice of any of these fine heavenly occupations."

"Thank you, God," said Amelio. "I am most honoured. But would you have an opening for a landscape artist?"

"Let me look again," said God. "Well, there is nothing like that available at this time. But why don't I create a job for you in the Glorious Sunrise Department? Would you like that?"

"I would love it," said Amelio.

"Then you shall have it!" said God. "But before you start, would you paint one of your famous rainbows on my face?"

"Of course!" replied Amelio.

And so, after a lifetime of hard work, Amelio was at last able to create great landscapes. And one morning, if you are up early enough . . .

. . . you may have the good fortune to see some of his fine work.

THE AUTHOR

John Bianchi is an author/illustrator with almost 20 children's books to his credit. His best known works include *Princess Frownsalot, The Swine Snafu, Penelope Penguin: The Incredibly Good Baby* and *Snowed In At Pokeweed Public School.*

His books with creative partner Frank B. Edwards include *Mortimer Mooner Stopped Taking a Bath* and *Snow: Learning For The Fun Of It.*

The pair formed Bungalo Books in 1986 and gave up serious employment shortly after so that they could pursue their love of children's books on a full-time basis.